Understanding and Managing PDA in Children

Empowering Parents and Educators to Guide Kids
with Pathological Demand Avoidance (Autism)
Through Triggers, Meltdowns to Success

Linda Horton

1

Table of Contents

Introduction

Pathological Demand Avoidance (PDA) presents a fascinating yet challenging dimension within the vast landscape of autism spectrum disorders (ASD). The term itself encapsulates a complex interplay of behaviors and cognitive patterns that significantly impact the lives of those affected. It is crucial to establish a solid foundation for comprehending PDA by examining its etymology and historical context within the broader field of autism research.

Delving into the essence of PDA requires a nuanced exploration of its defining characteristics. At its core, PDA is marked by an intricate dance between the individual's intense need for control and a pervasive avoidance of external demands. Unlike other forms of autism, this avoidance is not rooted in defiance or a desire to be oppositional but, rather, it emerges as a coping mechanism intertwined with anxiety and a profound discomfort with expectations.

To truly grasp the significance of PDA, it is imperative to position it within the larger framework of autism spectrum disorders. While individuals with PDA share certain core features with other forms of autism, such as difficulties in social interaction and repetitive behaviors, the distinctiveness of PDA lies in its manifestation through a heightened resistance to demands. This resistance often leads to disruptions in daily life, impacting not only the individual but also those within their immediate social circle.

The journey of understanding PDA commences with the ability to recognize its subtle manifestations in early childhood. Parents and caregivers are the frontline observers, tasked with deciphering signs that may indicate a predisposition towards PDA. These signs may encompass a heightened sensitivity to changes in routine, extreme emotional responses to seemingly trivial demands, and challenges with transitions. Early recognition becomes a cornerstone for timely interventions that can significantly alter the trajectory of a child's development.

As the narrative of PDA unfolds, the role of parents and educators emerges as pivotal in shaping the trajectory of individuals affected by this profile. Parental involvement extends beyond traditional caregiving; it transforms into advocacy and emotional scaffolding for the child. Similarly, educators become architects of tailored learning environments, necessitating an in-depth understanding of the unique challenges presented by PDA. Together, parents and educators form a symbiotic partnership, essential for the holistic well-being of the individual.

Navigating the complexities of PDA requires more than individual efforts; it demands the creation of a robust support network. Families grappling with the challenges of PDA find solace and strength in connecting with others who share similar experiences. Support groups, both online and offline, serve as invaluable forums for sharing strategies, discussing coping mechanisms, and fostering a sense of community. This network not only offers emotional support but also serves as a repository of practical wisdom drawn from collective experiences.

The collaborative journey extends to the realm of professionals who specialize in autism spectrum disorders. Engaging with clinicians, psychologists, and educators becomes a dynamic process of assessment, intervention, and ongoing support. Professionals bring a wealth of expertise to the table, conducting comprehensive assessments that delve into the intricacies of an individual's cognitive and behavioral profile. The collaboration goes beyond diagnosis, extending into the crafting of personalized intervention plans that address the unique needs of individuals with PDA.

Chapter 1

Unraveling the Complexity of PDA

Exploring the Spectrum of Autism Disorders

Autism spectrum disorders (ASD) form a diverse array of neurodevelopmental conditions, each presenting a unique set of challenges. Within this spectrum, Pathological Demand Avoidance (PDA) stands out due to its distinctive characteristics. Autism, encompassing a spectrum of symptoms related to social interaction, communication, and repetitive behaviors, provides a foundational context for understanding the complexity of PDA. PDA, however, introduces additional challenges, marked notably by an aversion to demands and a compelling need for control.

The spectrum itself spans from conditions like Asperger's syndrome, characterized by structured behaviors, to classic autism with severe communication and social interaction impairments. PDA, occupying a distinct place, demands a deeper exploration to unravel its complexities within the broader context of autism.

Differentiating PDA from Other Autism Profiles

Distinguishing PDA from other autism profiles necessitates a nuanced examination of behavioral nuances and responses to stimuli. While commonalities exist, such as social withdrawal and communication challenges, PDA introduces a layer of complexity related to avoidance of demands. It is crucial to recognize PDA as a unique manifestation within the broader autism spectrum, avoiding the trap of viewing it through a singular lens.

PDA shares some characteristics with oppositional defiant disorder (ODD), but the underlying motivation sets them apart. Unlike ODD, where defiance is primary,

PDA's resistance is rooted in anxiety-driven control needs. This distinction underscores the importance of tailored strategies in managing PDA, acknowledging that approaches effective for other autism profiles may require adaptation.

Psychological and Neurological Aspects of PDA

The complexity of PDA extends beyond observable behaviors, delving into the intricate interplay of psychological and neurological factors. Psychologically, individuals with PDA grapple with intense anxiety, often triggered by external demands. This anxiety, coupled with a need for control, shapes their behavioral responses. Cognitive rigidity in PDA is not mere stubbornness; it's a coping mechanism arising from heightened sensitivity to perceived threats.

Neurologically, PDA is associated with atypical patterns in brain function and connectivity. Research indicates altered neural responses to social cues and heightened reactivity to perceived demands in individuals with PDA. Understanding these neurological aspects is fundamental in tailoring interventions to address the root causes of PDA behaviors rather than merely mitigating their surface manifestations.

Chapter 2

Identifying Triggers and Stressors

Environmental Factors Contributing to PDA

In the intricate landscape of Pathological Demand Avoidance (PDA), a crucial aspect lies in discerning the environmental factors that wield a profound influence on individuals navigating this unique profile within the autism spectrum. The environment, whether it be the familiar setting of home, the structured surroundings of school, or the dynamic landscape of the broader community, acts as a potent force in shaping the behaviors and responses of those with PDA. The significance lies in recognizing that environmental elements can act as triggers, catalyzing heightened stress and avoidance behaviors.

Consider the scenario where routine, a stabilizing force for many, undergoes unexpected changes. For an individual with PDA, this disruption can become a potent stressor, unleashing a cascade of anxiety-driven responses. The lack of predictability in the environment becomes not just a challenge but a trigger for avoidance behaviors. Therefore, a nuanced examination of the environment becomes imperative in understanding and mitigating the impact of these triggers, fostering a sense of security and stability.

Moreover, the social environment within these broader settings plays a pivotal role in contributing to the complexities of PDA. Social interactions, often perceived as routine and unremarkable, become potential sources of intense stress. An essential facet of environmental analysis involves scrutinizing the social dynamics at play. Group activities, crowded spaces, or even one-on-one interactions can become arenas where anxiety escalates, propelling individuals with PDA towards avoidance as a coping mechanism. Thus, a comprehensive understanding of environmental triggers lays the foundation for creating supportive surroundings conducive to minimizing stress and enhancing the overall well-being of those with PDA.

Social Interaction Challenges

The realm of social interactions unfolds as a multifaceted landscape of challenges for individuals navigating PDA. Within this intricate tapestry, the identification of triggers and stressors requires a deep dive into the nuanced dynamics of social engagement. For those with PDA, social interactions pose unique challenges that extend beyond the conventional hurdles associated with autism spectrum disorders. Here, the demand for social reciprocity becomes a salient stressor, requiring individuals to navigate the complex and often unspoken rules of social engagement.

In essence, the intricate nature of social interactions becomes a breeding ground for anxiety. The fear of making social errors, the pressure to conform to societal norms, and the complexities of non-verbal cues contribute to an overwhelming experience for individuals with PDA. By scrutinizing these social intricacies, caregivers, educators, and professionals can identify specific challenges acting as triggers for avoidance behaviors. This understanding becomes a cornerstone for crafting targeted interventions aimed at enhancing social communication skills and, consequently, alleviating the stress associated with social engagement.

Sensory Overload and PDA

Within the realm of PDA, the sensory landscape emerges as a critical arena for identifying triggers and stressors. Individuals with PDA often exhibit heightened sensitivities to sensory stimuli, ranging from the visual to the auditory and tactile domains. The experience of sensory overload becomes a significant contributor to the manifestation of avoidance behaviors, representing a coping mechanism to manage the overwhelming influx of sensory information.

In delving into the intricacies of sensory challenges, it is imperative to recognize the individualized nature of these triggers. A flickering fluorescent light, an abrupt loud noise, or the texture of a certain fabric—all these sensory stimuli can act as catalysts for heightened stress. Therefore, the process of identifying triggers involves mapping out these unique sensitivities, creating a sensory profile that serves as a guide for caregivers and educators. This comprehensive understanding empowers them to tailor environments to minimize sensory overload, providing individuals with PDA the tools to regulate their sensory experiences and reduce anxiety effectively.

Chapter 3

Understanding Meltdowns and Shutdowns

Behavioral Manifestations of PDA

Delving into the intricacies of Pathological Demand Avoidance (PDA) necessitates a profound exploration of the behavioral manifestations that characterize meltdowns and shutdowns within this unique profile of the autism spectrum. The manifestations of meltdowns and shutdowns in individuals with PDA are multifaceted, representing a complex interplay of anxiety, sensory sensitivities, and an overwhelming need for control.

Meltdowns, intense and often explosive, are marked by an escalation of stress that exceeds an individual's ability to cope. In the context of PDA, these meltdowns are not rooted in defiance but rather emerge as a response to an overwhelming sense of demands. The demand avoidance inherent in PDA, when confronted with situations perceived as challenging or threatening, can trigger a cascade of behaviors ranging from verbal outbursts to physical reactions.

Shutdowns, on the other hand, represent a withdrawal response where individuals retreat into themselves as a coping mechanism. It is an attempt to regain a sense of control and reduce sensory and emotional stimuli. The complexity lies in recognizing the subtle signs of shutdowns, which may include withdrawal, avoidance of eye contact, and a disengagement from the immediate environment.

Understanding these behavioral manifestations involves peeling back the layers to reveal the underlying triggers. The demand for flexibility or adherence to specific routines, unexpected changes, or sensory overload can all act as catalysts for meltdowns and shutdowns. Recognizing these triggers is foundational for caregivers, educators, and professionals to implement targeted strategies that prevent or mitigate the impact of these intense reactions.

Coping Mechanisms and Strategies

Within the realm of meltdowns and shutdowns, the exploration of coping mechanisms and strategies takes center stage. Coping mechanisms employed by individuals with PDA are adaptive responses to manage the overwhelming stressors that lead to meltdowns or shutdowns. Understanding these coping mechanisms is crucial for tailoring interventions that provide alternative avenues for individuals to navigate challenging situations.

One prevalent coping mechanism is the use of control as a means of reducing anxiety. Individuals with PDA may seek control over their environment or daily routines to create a predictable and manageable space. However, the delicate balance lies in recognizing when this need for control becomes a hindrance, exacerbating stress rather than alleviating it.

Another coping strategy involves avoidance—avoidance of situations perceived as demanding or threatening. While avoidance provides a temporary escape from stressors, it poses challenges in the long run, limiting exposure to situations essential for growth and development. Identifying these avoidance patterns is vital in developing targeted strategies that gradually expose individuals to manageable levels of demands, fostering adaptive coping mechanisms.

Social withdrawal can be a coping mechanism manifested through shutdowns. Individuals may withdraw from social interactions as a response to sensory or social overload. Recognizing these withdrawal patterns is key to implementing strategies that gradually build tolerance to social engagement while providing avenues for self-regulation.

Strategies for managing meltdowns involve creating predictable and structured environments that reduce anxiety. Visual schedules, clear communication of expectations, and the provision of sensory breaks can all contribute to minimizing stressors. Tailoring interventions to address the specific triggers of meltdowns and shutdowns is a dynamic process that requires ongoing observation, flexibility, and collaboration between caregivers, educators, and professionals.

Supporting Individuals During Meltdowns

Supporting individuals during meltdowns represents a delicate yet crucial aspect of navigating PDA. Meltdowns can be distressing not only for the individual but also for those in their immediate surroundings. Understanding how to provide support during these intense moments requires a combination of empathy, patience, and a deep awareness of individual triggers.

Firstly, it is essential to recognize the signs leading up to a meltdown or shutdown. Changes in behavior, heightened anxiety, or sensory sensitivities can serve as precursors. Early identification provides an opportunity for preemptive strategies, potentially averting the escalation into a full-blown meltdown.

When a meltdown occurs, creating a calm and safe environment becomes paramount. This involves minimizing sensory stimuli, offering a designated space for self-regulation, and ensuring a supportive presence without imposing demands. Verbal communication during meltdowns may be limited, so nonverbal cues and gestures can serve as effective means of expressing support.

Moreover, post-meltdown support is crucial for individuals to regain equilibrium. Offering reassurance, validating their emotions, and providing opportunities for self-reflection contribute to the overall coping process. Collaborative debriefing, when appropriate, allows individuals to express their feelings and preferences, fostering a sense of agency and self-awareness.

Chapter 4

Effective Communication Strategies

Building a Language Bridge with PDA

Effective communication strategies form the cornerstone of navigating the unique challenges posed by Pathological Demand Avoidance (PDA). Building a language bridge with individuals exhibiting PDA involves a multifaceted approach that considers the nuanced aspects of communication inherent in this profile within the autism spectrum.

One of the key considerations in building this language bridge is recognizing the individualized nature of communication preferences. PDA manifests in a variety of ways, impacting verbal and nonverbal communication styles. Some individuals may experience difficulties expressing themselves verbally, while others may struggle with nonverbal cues. Therefore, the first step in effective communication is acknowledging and respecting the diversity within PDA.

Building a language bridge also involves fostering an environment that encourages communication without imposing demands. Traditional communication methods that rely heavily on direct questioning or authoritative directives may be counterproductive for individuals with PDA. Instead, adopting a collaborative and flexible communication style allows for meaningful engagement while minimizing anxiety associated with demands.

Moreover, incorporating the individual's interests and preferences into communication fosters a sense of connection. This personalized approach recognizes the importance of building rapport and trust, essential components of effective communication with individuals navigating PDA.

Nonverbal Communication in PDA

Nonverbal communication plays a pivotal role in the intricate dance of interaction with individuals experiencing PDA. Understanding and interpreting nonverbal cues become crucial, given that verbal communication may present challenges for some individuals within this profile. Nonverbal communication encompasses a spectrum of cues, including facial expressions, body language, gestures, and tone of voice.

For those with PDA, decoding nonverbal cues may be challenging due to heightened sensitivities or difficulties in interpreting social nuances. Therefore, effective communication strategies involve a two-fold approach refining one's own nonverbal communication to be clear and consistent while also recognizing and accommodating the unique nonverbal cues of individuals with PDA.

Creating a supportive environment that reduces sensory stimuli enhances the effectiveness of nonverbal communication. This involves being mindful of the physical space, lighting, and other sensory factors that may impact the individual's ability to attend to nonverbal cues. Establishing a sense of predictability in the environment contributes to the individual's comfort and facilitates better engagement in nonverbal communication.

Furthermore, incorporating visual supports, such as visual schedules or cues, can aid in comprehension. These supports serve as additional communication tools, providing a visual context that complements verbal and nonverbal interactions. The synergy between verbal and nonverbal communication creates a comprehensive language bridge that facilitates meaningful connections.

Tailoring Communication for Success

Tailoring communication strategies for success involves a dynamic process of adaptation and responsiveness to the individual's unique needs. It requires an in-depth understanding of the specific challenges and preferences within the spectrum of PDA. One size does not fit all, and effective communication necessitates a personalized and flexible approach.

Adapting communication to the individual's sensory profile is a key aspect of tailoring strategies for success. Recognizing sensitivities to certain sounds, textures, or visual stimuli allows communicators to create environments conducive to effective engagement. Moreover, being attentive to the individual's preferred communication mode—whether it be verbal, written, or visual—ensures that the communication bridge is constructed on a foundation of comfort and accessibility.

Additionally, employing a positive and strengths-based communication style fosters a sense of empowerment. Acknowledging and reinforcing the individual's strengths and accomplishments builds confidence and motivation to engage in communication. Positive reinforcement serves as a powerful tool in shaping communication behaviors, emphasizing successful interactions and fostering a willingness to participate in future communication exchanges.

Implementing clear and unambiguous language also contributes to successful communication. Ambiguity or vague language can be anxiety-inducing for individuals with PDA, potentially leading to avoidance or misinterpretation. Therefore, using concrete language, providing clear instructions, and avoiding unnecessary ambiguity enhance the clarity of communication and reduce stress associated with uncertainty.

Chapter 5

Educational Approaches and Strategies

Creating an Inclusive Learning Environment

The realm of education for individuals with Pathological Demand Avoidance (PDA) necessitates a paradigm shift towards creating an inclusive learning environment. This transformative approach goes beyond traditional models, recognizing the diverse needs and strengths of individuals within the spectrum of PDA. Building an inclusive learning environment involves a multifaceted strategy that considers the unique profile of PDA, fostering a space where individuals can thrive academically, socially, and emotionally.

Inclusivity begins with understanding the varied learning styles and preferences within PDA. The demand avoidance characteristic of PDA necessitates a departure from conventional teaching methods that heavily rely on directives and rigid structures. Instead, educators can adopt a flexible approach that accommodates individualized learning styles, allowing for a balance between structure and adaptability.

Sensory considerations play a crucial role in creating an inclusive environment. Individuals with PDA may experience sensory sensitivities that impact their ability to engage in the learning process. Modifying the physical environment, such as minimizing sensory stimuli and providing sensory breaks, contributes to a more supportive atmosphere. Tailoring instructional materials to accommodate sensory preferences ensures that individuals can fully participate in the educational experience.

Furthermore, promoting social inclusivity is vital. Peer relationships and social interactions are integral components of the educational journey. Educators can implement strategies that foster understanding and empathy among peers, creating a positive social dynamic. Peer support systems contribute to a sense of belonging, reducing social anxiety and promoting collaborative learning.

Individualized Education Plans (IEPs) for PDA

The development and implementation of Individualized Education Plans (IEPs) represent a cornerstone in addressing the unique educational needs of individuals with PDA. An IEP is a personalized roadmap that outlines specific goals, accommodations, and support strategies tailored to the individual's learning profile. For those with PDA, crafting a comprehensive and dynamic IEP is paramount for fostering academic success and personal growth.

The first step in formulating an effective IEP involves a thorough assessment of the individual's strengths, challenges, and preferences. This assessment provides a foundation for setting realistic and attainable goals that align with the individual's developmental trajectory. Recognizing the individualized nature of PDA ensures that the IEP is tailored to address specific demand avoidance patterns, sensory sensitivities, and social communication challenges.

Accommodations within the IEP focus on creating an environment that minimizes stressors and maximizes learning potential. For instance, incorporating flexible scheduling to accommodate changes in routine or providing access to sensory breaks can enhance the individual's ability to engage in the learning process. Additionally, modifying assessment methods to align with the individual's preferred mode of expression allows for a more accurate evaluation of academic progress.

Regular review and modification of the IEP are essential components of its effectiveness. The dynamic nature of PDA requires a flexible and responsive approach, with educators and support professionals collaborating to adapt strategies based on ongoing observations and assessments. The IEP serves as a living document that evolves alongside the individual's growth and development.

Collaborative Teaching Techniques

Collaborative teaching techniques represent a dynamic approach to fostering an inclusive and supportive educational environment for individuals with PDA. This approach transcends traditional models by emphasizing teamwork among educators, support professionals, and caregivers. The collaboration extends to peers, creating a unified network dedicated to the success and well-being of the individual with PDA.

Within a collaborative teaching framework, open communication is paramount. Educators and support professionals share insights, observations, and strategies to ensure a cohesive and consistent approach to addressing the unique needs of the individual. Regular meetings provide a platform for discussing progress, challenges, and adjustments to instructional methods, fostering a collective understanding of the dynamic nature of PDA.

Inclusive education involves the active participation of all stakeholders, including peers. Peers can contribute significantly to the learning experience by fostering a supportive and empathetic environment. Educators can implement strategies such as peer mentoring, cooperative learning activities, and awareness campaigns to promote understanding and acceptance among classmates.

Moreover, collaborative teaching extends beyond the classroom to include collaboration with professionals specializing in PDA. Psychologists, speech therapists, and occupational therapists contribute valuable expertise to the educational team. This multidisciplinary approach ensures that the individual receives holistic support, addressing not only academic needs but also social, emotional, and sensory considerations.

Chapter 6

Collaborative Parenting Techniques

Parenting Challenges Specific to PDA

Navigating the realm of parenting a child with Pathological Demand Avoidance (PDA) introduces a unique set of challenges that demand a collaborative and adaptive approach. Understanding these challenges is foundational to the development of effective parenting techniques tailored to the distinctive nature of PDA.

One prominent challenge is the pervasive nature of demand avoidance exhibited by individuals with PDA. Unlike traditional defiance, demand avoidance in PDA stems from an anxiety-driven need for control. Parents often find themselves grappling with the delicate balance of setting necessary boundaries while recognizing and addressing the anxiety that demands may induce. This challenge requires parents to adopt strategies that minimize stressors and provide alternative avenues for their child to assert control in a constructive manner.

Another challenge is the heightened sensitivity to sensory stimuli, which can contribute to meltdowns and shutdowns. Parents may find themselves navigating unexpected triggers in various environments. Understanding and mitigating sensory sensitivities become crucial aspects of parenting a child with PDA. Creating sensory-friendly spaces at home, establishing predictable routines, and collaborating with educators to implement similar strategies at school contribute to a more supportive environment for the child.

Additionally, social communication challenges pose a hurdle in parent-child interactions. Individuals with PDA may struggle with interpreting social cues, expressing emotions, or engaging in reciprocal conversations. This challenge necessitates a nuanced parenting approach that prioritizes clear communication, visual supports, and the cultivation of social skills in a supportive and understanding environment.

Positive Reinforcement and Behavior Modification

Effective parenting techniques for children with PDA often revolve around positive reinforcement and behavior modification strategies. Traditional disciplinary methods may prove counterproductive, as demands and punishments can exacerbate anxiety and trigger avoidance behaviors. Positive reinforcement focuses on encouraging desired behaviors through rewards, recognition, and praise, fostering a more constructive and positive environment.

Identifying and reinforcing specific behaviors that align with expectations is a key aspect of positive reinforcement. This involves acknowledging and praising efforts and achievements, no matter how small. For instance, if a child successfully navigates a challenging social interaction, providing positive feedback reinforces the development of social communication skills.

Behavior modification strategies emphasize the gradual shaping of behaviors through consistent and positive interventions. Understanding the triggers for demand avoidance and employing proactive measures to address these triggers contribute to behavior modification. This may involve creating visual schedules to outline expectations, providing choices to empower the child, and gradually exposing them to manageable levels of demands to build tolerance over time.

Consistency is paramount in positive reinforcement and behavior modification. Parents play a crucial role in maintaining a consistent and supportive approach across different environments. Collaborating with educators, caregivers, and professionals involved in the child's life ensures a unified strategy that reinforces positive behaviors and minimizes stressors associated with demands.

Fostering Independence and Self-Regulation

Fostering independence and self-regulation represents a cornerstone in parenting techniques for children with PDA. Building these skills empowers the child to navigate challenges, make choices, and develop a sense of control in their daily lives. It also contributes to the reduction of demand avoidance behaviors by providing alternative means for the child to assert control in a constructive manner.

Encouraging independence involves gradually introducing tasks and responsibilities that align with the child's abilities. Breaking down larger tasks into smaller, manageable steps allows the child to experience success and build confidence. For example, establishing a routine for morning tasks or homework provides a structured framework that fosters independence.

Self-regulation skills are pivotal in helping children with PDA manage stress, sensory sensitivities, and emotional responses. Collaborative parenting techniques involve teaching and reinforcing self-regulation strategies tailored to the individual's needs. This may include sensory breaks, deep-breathing exercises, or the use of visual cues to signal when the child needs a moment to self-regulate.

Collaboration with educators is crucial in extending these skills to the school environment. Sharing successful strategies and reinforcing consistency between home and school settings contributes to the child's overall development of independence and self-regulation. Parent-teacher communication becomes a collaborative effort in addressing challenges and celebrating successes in fostering these essential skills.

Chapter 7

Therapeutic Interventions

Behavioral Therapies for PDA

Behavioral therapies emerge as instrumental components in the comprehensive approach to addressing the challenges associated with Pathological Demand Avoidance (PDA). These therapeutic interventions focus on modifying and shaping behaviors, with a nuanced understanding of the demand avoidance patterns inherent in PDA.

Applied Behavior Analysis (ABA) is a prominent behavioral therapy used in the context of PDA. ABA employs systematic and evidence-based strategies to reinforce desired behaviors and decrease challenging behaviors. For individuals with PDA, ABA can be adapted to target specific demand avoidance patterns by gradually exposing the individual to demands in a controlled and supportive manner. The emphasis on positive reinforcement, clear expectations, and consistency aligns with the core principles of ABA.

Another behavioral therapy that proves beneficial for individuals with PDA is Cognitive Behavioral Therapy (CBT). CBT focuses on the relationship between thoughts, feelings, and behaviors, providing individuals with tools to recognize and modify maladaptive thought patterns. In the context of PDA, CBT can address anxiety-driven thoughts that contribute to demand avoidance behaviors. By fostering self-awareness and coping strategies, CBT becomes a valuable therapeutic tool in managing the emotional aspects associated with PDA.

Social Skills Training is a behavioral therapy specifically designed to enhance social communication skills. Given the social communication challenges inherent in PDA, social skills training becomes an essential intervention. This therapy involves explicit instruction, modeling, and practice of social interactions. Tailoring social skills training to the individual's specific challenges, such as interpreting social cues or navigating group dynamics, contributes to the development of effective communication skills.

Occupational and Sensory Therapies

Occupational and sensory therapies play pivotal roles in addressing the sensory sensitivities and self-regulation challenges associated with PDA. These therapeutic interventions recognize the intricate interplay between sensory experiences, behavior, and overall well-being.

Occupational therapy focuses on developing and enhancing the individual's ability to participate in daily activities. For individuals with PDA, occupational therapy can address challenges related to fine and gross motor skills, coordination, and self-care routines. By tailoring interventions to the specific needs and preferences of the individual, occupational therapy contributes to increased independence and functional abilities.

Sensory integration therapy is particularly beneficial for individuals with PDA, who often experience heightened sensitivities to sensory stimuli. This therapy aims to help individuals process and respond to sensory information more effectively. Activities that expose the individual to different sensory stimuli in a controlled and gradual manner contribute to desensitization and improved sensory regulation. Sensory integration therapy aligns with the goal of creating sensory-friendly environments that minimize triggers for demand avoidance behaviors.

Moreover, the incorporation of sensory breaks within daily routines becomes a practical application of sensory therapies. These breaks provide individuals with PDA the opportunity to self-regulate and manage sensory overload. Collaborative efforts between occupational therapists, educators, and parents ensure that sensory strategies are consistent across various settings, creating a supportive and accommodating environment.

Role of Medication in PDA Management

The role of medication in managing Pathological Demand Avoidance (PDA) is a complex consideration that requires careful evaluation and collaboration between healthcare professionals and families. While medication is not a direct treatment for PDA, it can be prescribed to address specific symptoms or comorbid conditions that may exacerbate demand avoidance behaviors.

Individuals with PDA may experience coexisting conditions such as anxiety, depression, or attention-deficit/hyperactivity disorder (ADHD). In such cases, medications targeting these conditions may be considered as part of a comprehensive treatment plan. For example, selective serotonin reuptake inhibitors (SSRIs) or serotonin-norepinephrine reuptake inhibitors (SNRIs) may be prescribed to alleviate symptoms of anxiety or depression.

Attention to comorbid conditions extends to managing sensory sensitivities and hyperactivity. Medications such as antipsychotics or stimulants may be considered when sensory challenges or hyperactivity significantly impact the individual's daily functioning. It is crucial to approach medication management with an individualized perspective, carefully weighing the potential benefits and risks for each specific case.

Collaboration between healthcare professionals, including psychiatrists and pediatricians, and parents is integral in determining the appropriateness of medication. Ongoing monitoring and adjustments based on the individual's response and any potential side effects are essential aspects of medication management in the context of PDA.

Chapter 8

Transitioning to Adulthood

Preparing for Adolescence with PDA

The transition from adolescence to adulthood is a significant milestone for individuals with Pathological Demand Avoidance (PDA), marking a period of increased independence, self-discovery, and evolving responsibilities. Preparing for adolescence with PDA involves a proactive and individualized approach that considers the unique challenges and strengths within this developmental stage.

As adolescents with PDA navigate the complexities of adolescence, the demand avoidance patterns may manifest differently, influenced by hormonal changes, increased social expectations, and heightened self-awareness. Parents, educators, and professionals play pivotal roles in creating a supportive environment that addresses these challenges while fostering the autonomy and self-expression essential for healthy development.

Communication becomes a focal point during this transition. Open and transparent communication channels between adolescents with PDA and their support network are vital. This involves providing opportunities for the adolescent to express their preferences, concerns, and aspirations. Establishing a collaborative decision-making process empowers the individual, promoting a sense of agency in shaping their path to adulthood.

Additionally, preparing for adolescence involves addressing evolving social dynamics. Adolescents with PDA may encounter increased social expectations, peer relationships, and potential romantic interests. Social skills training and explicit guidance on navigating social nuances contribute to the development of meaningful connections. Creating social opportunities in controlled settings allows for the gradual integration of these skills into real-world scenarios.

Vocational and Life Skills Training

Vocational and life skills training form essential components of the transition to adulthood for individuals with PDA. As they prepare to enter the workforce and engage in independent living, acquiring practical skills becomes paramount. Vocational training focuses on developing the skills necessary for meaningful employment, considering the individual's strengths, interests, and capabilities.

Identifying vocational interests and strengths is a foundational step in vocational training for individuals with PDA. This involves conducting assessments, exploring potential career paths, and tailoring training programs to align with the individual's aptitudes. Recognizing that demand avoidance patterns may impact workplace dynamics, vocational training also addresses strategies for managing stressors and communication challenges in professional settings.

Life skills training encompasses a broader range of skills essential for independent living. This includes financial literacy, time management, organization, and daily living tasks. For individuals with PDA, who may experience challenges in planning and organization, life skills training provides structured guidance to enhance their ability to navigate the demands of daily life.

Furthermore, vocational and life skills training extend beyond the individual to include education and support for parents, caregivers, and educators. Collaborative efforts ensure a consistent and reinforcing approach, promoting the integration of learned skills into various aspects of the individual's life.

Independent Living and Community Integration

The transition to adulthood for individuals with PDA includes a focus on independent living and community integration. Independent living involves equipping individuals with the skills and resources necessary to manage their own living arrangements, make informed decisions, and cultivate a sense of autonomy.

Creating a pathway to independent living begins with assessing the individual's current capabilities and gradually expanding their skills. This may involve developing strategies for managing household tasks, grocery shopping, meal preparation, and self-care routines. Tailoring these skills to align with the individual's preferences and strengths ensures a meaningful and achievable transition to independent living.

Community integration is a parallel aspect that involves facilitating the individual's participation in community activities, social events, and recreational pursuits. This not only enhances their quality of life but also fosters a sense of belonging and connection. Identifying community resources, support networks, and opportunities for social engagement contributes to a holistic approach to transitioning to adulthood.

Moreover, preparing individuals with PDA for community integration involves addressing potential challenges in social communication. Social skills training and exposure to social scenarios in a supportive and controlled environment contribute to increased confidence and competence in navigating community interactions. Encouraging involvement in community groups, clubs, or volunteer opportunities further enhances social integration.

Collaboration between parents, educators, and professionals is integral in the process of independent living and community integration. This collaborative effort ensures a coordinated approach that addresses the multifaceted aspects of transitioning to adulthood for individuals with PDA. Ongoing support, guidance, and adjustment of strategies contribute to the successful integration of vocational, life, and social skills into the fabric of independent living.

Conclusion

The conclusion of this exploration marks not an endpoint but a transition into a phase of sustained support and advocacy. The long-term journey for individuals with PDA extends beyond diagnosis and intervention; it encompasses a commitment to ongoing support that adapts to the evolving needs of the individual.

Long-term support involves a continuum of care that extends into adolescence, adulthood, and beyond. This includes regular reassessment of therapeutic interventions, adjustments in educational approaches, and collaboration with vocational and community support networks. Recognizing that the demand avoidance patterns may manifest differently in various life stages emphasizes the need for flexibility and responsiveness in long-term support strategies.

Advocacy becomes a cornerstone in ensuring that individuals with PDA have equitable access to opportunities, resources, and understanding within society. This involves challenging stereotypes, dispelling misconceptions, and fostering a culture of acceptance. Advocacy extends to educational institutions, workplaces, and public spaces, promoting an inclusive environment that values the diverse strengths and contributions of individuals with PDA.

Moreover, long-term support and advocacy involve nurturing self-advocacy skills within individuals with PDA. Empowering them to express their needs, preferences, and aspirations fosters a sense of agency and autonomy. This journey is not one navigated solely by parents, educators, or professionals but is a collaborative effort that actively includes the voices and perspectives of individuals with PDA themselves.

Empowering the Future

Empowering the future for individuals with Pathological Demand Avoidance (PDA) involves a commitment to breaking barriers and creating pathways for success. Breaking barriers begins with dispelling myths and misconceptions surrounding PDA. It involves challenging preconceived notions that may hinder understanding and acceptance within society.

Education emerges as a powerful tool in breaking barriers. The dissemination of accurate and nuanced information about PDA within educational institutions, training programs, and community forums contributes to a more informed and empathetic society. Educators play a pivotal role in this process, becoming advocates for inclusive practices and supportive environments that embrace neurodiversity.

Breaking barriers extends to the realm of employment. Individuals with PDA possess unique strengths, talents, and perspectives that can enrich workplaces. Fostering an inclusive and accommodating work environment involves recognizing and leveraging these strengths. Implementing workplace accommodations and providing education on neurodiversity contribute to breaking down employment barriers for individuals with PDA.

The broader community is a crucial ally in breaking barriers. Community engagement initiatives, awareness campaigns, and collaborative projects create opportunities for meaningful interaction between individuals with PDA and the community. Breaking barriers involves fostering a sense of belonging, reducing stigma, and promoting a culture of acceptance within neighborhoods, social groups, and public spaces.